WOMAN
WIFE
MOTHER

by
Pat Harrison

HARRISON HOUSE
Tulsa, Oklahoma

Woman, Wife, Mother
ISBN 0-89274-862-1
(Former ISBN 0-89274-315-8)
Copyright © 1984, 1991 by Pat Harrison
P. O. Box 35443
Tulsa, Oklahoma 74153

Published by Harrison House, Inc.
P. O. Box 35035
Tulsa, Oklahoma 74153

Contents

Foreword

Having known the author of this book in a very personal and intimate way for over 30 years, I feel qualified to say whether she knows what she is writing about. In short, she does!

As a woman, she fills the role with all the grace, dignity and class that God could bestow upon an individual.

As a wife, she has done everything within her ability and knowledge to minister to me in every area: spirit, soul and body.

As a mother, she is the finest—the result being three children who excel in quality.

Because of her standards as a wife and mother, she has never been a shame or disappointment to us.

I salute you, Mrs. Harrison. You are one of the greatest! And you, the reader, will surely be blessed.

— Buddy Harrison

PART I
God's Intent
For Woman

1

A Bible Look at
Woman, Wife, and Mother

Every woman, whether single, married, or divorced, can profit from a study of what the Word of God has to say on the subject of woman, wife, and mother. If single now, perhaps you will be involved as a wife and mother someday. If not, you can still minister to others by gaining knowledge on this topic. There is always counseling to be done; and when you get women to realize how beautiful it is that God created them women, that settles many problems. Those whose children are gone from home can learn things that will minister life to their grandchildren.

The second chapter of Genesis gives us insight into the creation of woman. I believe that by studying this portion of Scripture, women will be thrilled when they see that God saw fit to create them women.

Let's begin with Genesis 2:7:

> **Then the Lord God formed man of the dust of the ground, and breathed into his nostrils the breath or spirit of life; and man became a living being.**

> **And the Lord God planted a garden toward the east in Eden (meaning delight); and there He put the man whom He had formed (framed, constituted).**

> **And out of the ground the Lord God made to grow every tree that is pleasant to the sight or to be desired, good, (suitable, pleasant) for food; the tree of life also in the center of the garden, and the tree of knowledge of [the difference between] good and evil, and blessing and calamity.**
>
> **Genesis 2:7-9 AMP**

9

Now let's skip to the fifteenth verse:

> And the Lord God took the man and put him in the garden of Eden to tend and guard and keep it.

> And the Lord God commanded the man, saying, You may freely eat of every tree of the garden,

> Except of the tree of the knowledge of good and evil and of blessing and calamity you shall not eat, for in the day that you eat of it you shall surely die.

> Now the Lord God said, It is not good [sufficient, satisfactory] that the man should be alone; I will make him a helper meet (suitable, adapted, completing) for him.

> Genesis 2:15-18 AMP

The Scripture goes on to tell how God formed the animals and beasts and let Adam name them. But God still saw that for Adam there was not a helper who was adaptable, suitable, and completing for him. So in Genesis 2:21-25 we are told:

> And the Lord God caused a deep sleep to fall upon Adam, and while he slept He took one of his ribs—a part of his side—and closed up the [place with] flesh instead of it;

> And the rib or part of his side which the Lord God had taken from the man, He built up and made into a woman and brought her to the man.

> Then Adam said, This [creature] is now bone of my bones and flesh of my flesh. She shall be called Woman, because she was taken out of a man.

> Therefore a man shall leave his father and his mother and shall become united and cleave to his wife, and they shall become one flesh.

> And the man and his wife were both naked, and were not embarrassed or ashamed in each other's presence.

> Genesis 2:21-25 AMP

I want to lay a foundation here, so you can see some differences between man and woman. Genesis 2:7 tells us God formed man. In the original Hebrew, one definition of being formed is "squeezed together." That is why man, many times, appears rugged.

But in verse 22, where we are told about God creating woman, the Hebrew means "skillfully and carefully handcrafted."

The Lord showed me that this was so a woman would be desired and admired.

God says this woman was to be a "helper meet." The word *help* means "to give aid and assistance," and the word *meet* means "to surround." You could say the woman is to continually surround with aid and assistance.

That is what you are as a helper meet. You are skillfully and carefully handcrafted to be suitable, adaptable, and completing to a man. The way you become those things is by continually surrounding the one God has given you with aid and assistance.

Once you've accepted yourself as a woman, you are proud because your Creator saw fit to create you. He saw that you could flow and walk in that to perfection. God sees every creation as good and perfect—and that's how you're to see yourself! When you see yourself that way, you will see your mate that way. That's important. You weren't made for man to see himself differently than how God made him, but you were created to make yourself adaptable, suitable, and completing for him.

We read in Genesis 2:24 AMP, "Therefore a man shall leave his father and his mother and shall become united and cleave to his wife, and they shall become one flesh."

The word *cleave* in the Hebrew means "to never stop chasing." If you, as the woman, continually surround your husband with aid and assistance, he will never stop chasing you! You are making him complete at all times; therefore, he desires to be around you. He always desires to have you with him so he is complete.

11

The Church has a relationship with Jesus which parallels that between husband and wife. We are the Church, the Bride, and He is the Bridegroom. When we look to Him, and go forth doing what we are placed on this earth to do, then He meets our every need. But when we're not going forth, being His arms extended, there is that sense of not feeling Him around us—not being aware He is there.

When you, as a woman (because you were created for man), do not function as you should, making yourself suitable, adaptable, and completing for your husband, you don't have the sense of fulfillment that is needed for him. That's because you're not doing what you're supposed to be doing.

You have a big responsibility. It is important that you function as God created you. Woman was created perfect— not just for God, but for man. That was lost in the Garden when Adam sold out to Satan, but through Jesus it has been restored. And through that restoration, through spiritual adoption in Jesus Christ, we can again be the perfect woman God created us to be. We are that unto God and man.

The Bible tells us that God placed the Tree of Life in the middle of the Garden. It was the Tree of Life which kept Adam and Eve perfect. Today we can see the parallel in Jesus. He is the tree of life to us. By always feeding upon Jesus, the Word, we dwell and continue in our perfection in Him. We know who we are in Christ, and we can be just as He expects us to be. We can do just as He expects us to do. He is the One Who brought back the perfection that was lost in the Garden.

The Word tells us that when we accept Jesus we are a new creation. Our spirit, the real us, is perfect. This spirit within us makes us function and be perfected as we should here on this earth. We have to realize that, and walk in it. It's important to meditate on the Word in these areas.

12

Sometimes we have difficulty with a certain thing. We think, "Why is this becoming so hard for me?" Then we realize we've not been meditating in the Word as we should. It's not that we've lost the Word, but we've lost our awareness of it. We haven't been speaking it out. When we hear the Word, it penetrates within and becomes a reality. When it's spoken out, the manifestation is complete. The Word has to be a part of us, but that will not happen until we feed on it continually.

We cannot receive strength and nourishment from food by simply sitting and looking at it every day at mealtime. But people will look at the Word and think, *I don't know what that means.* They'll put it on the shelf. It would be the same way in the natural if we sat down at the table and said, "I can't tell if that food would do me any good."

The Word is not just paper and ink—it's life. And we need to be established through the Word on this subject of woman, wife, and mother.

Let's look at a New Testament scripture that shows again how woman was created for man.

> **Neither was man created on account of or for the benefit of woman, but woman on account of and for the benefit of man.**
>
> **Therefore she should [be subject to his authority and should] have a covering on her head [as a token, a symbol, of her submission] to authority, [that she may show reverence as do] the angels and not displease them.**
>
> **Nevertheless, in [the plan of] the Lord and from His point of view woman is not apart from and independent of man, nor is man aloof from and independent of woman;**
>
> **For as woman was made from man, even so man is also born of woman. And all [whether male or female go forth] from God (as their Author).**
>
> **1 Corinthians 11:9-12 AMP**

We see again why God created woman. First Corinthians 11:7 tells us man is the image and reflected glory of

God, and that woman is the expression of man's glory, his majesty, and preeminence. That's the reason we should respect the position he is in and honor him. In doing that, we cause him to be complete and to function on this earth as God intended.

That's part of our adapting and being suitable—part of our responsibility as a woman. The husband/wife relationship is not just something the world thought up. It's from God.

It is so important that before you marry you establish your relationship with the Father God. If you know Him intimately, then the natural laws which cause you to be effective to a man automatically fall into place. You have such a relationship and fellowship with God that you know how He created you and why, and you can flow in that. You know what you are supposed to do.

The Bible says we are to submit ourselves to our husbands. Submission is an attitude of the heart—not a physical action. That's why the Bible says to submit to your husband as to the Lord. (Eph. 5:22.) How do you submit yourself to Jesus? With an attitude of love.

In a marriage, you understand authority, you understand your husband's position, you understand submission—and you have no problem submitting.

You are not going to be a robot—but you and your husband will form a union. That is what God desires. Because you were made for man, you have a responsibility to look at marriage this way.

If we are submitted to Jesus and He is Lord of our life, we should not wonder what He can do for us, but we should ask, "What can we do for Him?" We can reach out and bring other people into balance by bringing them to Him, being ministers of reconciliation. We bring balance, too—and completion—to the marriage union.

Since we were also made for man, we need to see what we can do for him. That way, by adapting ourselves, and by making ourselves suitable and completing, we will reap the benefits of the law of giving and receiving.

Love never fails. And you do this through love. Your husband has to respond to love, because love draws—it never pushes away.

If in your marriage there are times you feel you're being separated or drawn away from your husband, don't get your eyes on the circumstances or your mate (saying he does this or that). Check up on yourself. The Lord can show you areas where you are not fulfilling your role as you should. When you begin to adapt, everything will come into perspective.

As women, because we have been classified as the weaker sex, we want to sit down and let man wait on us, put us up on a pedestal because we're delicate, and do things that are supposed to be done for a lady. But that isn't the way it is.

Man and woman are equal in the sight of God. He created you for man; you're strong. You are perfect in the Lord Jesus Christ.

So be suitable, adaptable, and completing to your husband, continually surrounding him with aid and assistance. In that way, you will be following the role of woman that God created you for. You will be the joy your husband desires, and yes, you will be the only person in his life. And He will lift you up.

When my husband knew I wouldn't be home on my birthday, he sent me a beautiful bouquet of two dozen pink roses with a precious note that read, "Even though we're apart, we're together, and you excel them all." That made me know the Word was working in my life.

2

A True Wife and Mother

The book of Proverbs has much to say about women and men. Proverbs 18:22 AMP says, "He who finds a [true] wife finds a good thing, and obtains favor of the Lord." What is a true wife? She is a helper meet—someone who makes herself suitable, adaptable, and completing for her husband. She can do that because she has done it for her Creator. She's already had spiritual fellowship and intimacy with Him, so she can flow in it in the natural.

If you're not a true wife, you won't be "a good thing." You won't have favor of the Lord because your actions and words will keep your husband from functioning as he should in God's will. He will be trying to please you to keep peace. He no longer will be following God, but following you. Therefore, he will not obtain favor from the Lord.

Now let's look at another scripture, Proverbs 12:4 AMP. The first of this verse reads: "A virtuous and worthy wife—earnest and strong in character—is a crowning joy to her husband . . . ."

Strong's Exhaustive Concordance of the Bible says *crown* is a primary root word meaning to encircle for attack or protection; especially to compass. The dictionary definition of *crown* is "something that imparts splendor, honor, and finish; to bring to a successful conclusion; to culminate" (that means to bring to the highest point). The word *compass* means "to achieve, accomplish, and obtain." As a crowning joy, you are a virtuous and worthy wife, earnest and strong in character, a thing of splendor, honor, and finish to your husband. You cause him to reach the highest point. You cause him to achieve, accomplish, and obtain the perfect will of God in his life because you continually adapt yourself, make yourself suitable and completing for him, and surround him with aid and assistance. Then you are his crown and glory. You are his crown and joy, joy meaning the emotion evoked by well-being. You take care of your husband. Because you possess what he desires, he experiences great pleasure and delight.

I'm so thankful to God for creating me as a woman and making it possible for me to walk in that perfection. I can be a crown and joy to my husband, because God makes me virtuous and worthy. I make myself earnest and strong in character by meditating on the Word, by eating the Word, and by making the Word a part of me continually. That's what makes my character what it should be, because that is the character of God.

The second part of Proverbs 12:4 AMP says, ". . . but she who makes ashamed is as rottenness in his bones." I wouldn't want to be in that position. Being in the ministry, I've seen some ministers' wives who are like that, and I feel sorry for them. They're never happy, no matter what God or man does for them. They are often seeking after houses and riches, trying to find happiness in the natural realm.

Another Scripture passage on this same subject is Proverbs 19:14,15 AMP:

> **House and riches are the inheritance from fathers, but a wise, understanding and prudent wife is from the Lord.**
>
> **Slothfulness casts one into a deep sleep, and the idle person shall suffer hunger.**

This passage also shows that the slothful person is unwise and dissatisfied. A wife who is slothful or seeking happiness in the natural cannot help her husband be successful and attain to the highest.

She is the kind who will put him down with her words and actions. This is when she becomes "as rottenness in his bones." She will laugh at him in front of others and say, "Oh, he could never do anything right." She makes fun so much that the words of her mouth have penetrated until she has no respect for him. As a result, he has no respect for himself. He becomes (at least in her eyes) what she had thought.

She has kept her husband from reaching that highest point of achievement in his life. I don't want to be caught in that position.

Another Scripture that teaches along these same lines is Proverbs 21:9 AMP: "It is better to dwell in a corner of the housetop [on the flat, oriental roof, exposed to all kinds of weather] than in a house shared with a nagging, quarrelsome and faultfinding woman." You can't say it any plainer than that. At least if the husband were on the roof, he would be out of earshot from his wife and could keep his peace with God. He could keep his perspective and go on. Otherwise, he would become confused and not succeed as God had intended.

The blame for his failure will be on his wife's shoulders. God has told us we are to make ourselves virtuous and pure, earnest and strong. In doing that, we can function in perfection as the woman—spirit, soul, and body—that God created us to be.

Many times women don't want that kind of responsibility. But it's already there. So we might as well walk in it and reap the results of good seeds.

That's what I want to do. Because in that, I have within me a fulfillment, knowing I am not only pleasing God, but

I'm pleasing the man God gave me. All the time I'm still putting God first.

Often, as women, we have a tendency to be the opposite of what 1 Corinthians 13 (the love scripture) says. We get fretful and resentful.

Many times our husbands are out with the public during the day. When they come home, they don't want to go anywhere or do anything. Because we are made for them, we must make ourselves suitable and adaptable.

Realize that your husband has been out all day long with people who have badgered him, pulled him, and pushed him. He just wants to come back to the home God has given him, and he wants it to be peaceful and full of joy. It becomes peaceful by your being in your place and doing your part every day.

The first thing you need to do on a daily basis is pray and intercede for your husband. You can pray like this:

> Father, I thank You that this day Your life is within him. Because Your life is in him, he will flow in Your will this day. He will see people in need and be able to reach out and help them. He will be able to turn his back on those who are jeering at him and giving him problems. He will walk in success. He will be able to speak forth that which You desire, and he will not give in to the flesh.

Then you begin to intercede for your home:

> Father, I thank You that this day my home is perfected. I thank You that my children walk in peace, joy, and love.

If your children are in school, take authority over the evil forces that would try to come against them. Then stand your ground, knowing they are protected.

You must pray on a daily basis. Don't let things go until you feel an urgency in your spirit. Don't wait until Suzy is acting strange and you don't understand why. How long has it been since you prayed for her? It should be daily. That is part of keeping your home in order—full of joy, peace, love, and understanding.

In doing that, you are causing your spirit man to live big inside you. Your spirit is dominating, and you are acting according to it and not according to your feelings or the world's standards.

In this day and age, the big thing is "my ministry." Don't make the mistake of putting a ministry before your home. Everybody has a ministry. God says we are to reach out to people with the ministry of reconciliation. But that is not your personal ministry. It is the Church's ministry.

God created the home first. Even if He has called you to a ministry, it is not to be placed above your home. If you are putting your ministry before your husband or your children, you are out of the will of God. If there are no homes, there won't be any churches.

The devil would love to divide homes and split them up so there wouldn't be any churches. Without churches, we could not be bound together in ideal harmony.

A few years ago I was asked to speak at a ladies' luncheon in Florida. I had never been to that area and didn't know the people. One lady was obviously offended by something I said. I learned later that she had been involved in a teaching that was hard on women. For instance, they were not allowed to speak unless told to. She had come out from that bondage, but couldn't handle the freedom and had gone to the other extreme. She didn't have time for her husband, her children, or her housework.

Another lady told me, "I was never so shocked as when I went into her home. It was a mess—dirty dishes and dirty clothes everywhere. The woman came in just in time to go to a meeting and said to her husband, 'I'm sorry, you'll have to take the kids and get them something to eat; we have to go.'"

She had not been cooking meals. If the children got fed, it was the husband who took them to eat. If anything got washed, the husband did it. The wife didn't have time. She "had a ministry."

That is not the will of God for a wife. She was first made for God. She is to be in true fellowship with Him and know Him as He knows her.

Then she was made for man. Because her perspective is right with God, it will be right with her mate.

Don't put your children above your husband. Many couples get divorced later in life because the wife was so busy with her children, making sure they got everything they wanted, that she and her husband became almost strangers.

God didn't make you for your children. He made you for man. You would have no children if it weren't for your relationship with your husband. Your children are a result of the two of you becoming one flesh. First, you become one in spirit with your husband; then you become one in soul and body.

You reap the benefit of beautiful children. Teach them properly in the Word and live the Word before them. They will be a pleasure to you. But it won't happen if you put your children before your husband. Push him away and he will find other interests. Then when the children are gone, two people who don't know one another are left living in the same house. It's not a home; it's a house. Because it has been that way so many years, the two people don't even have a desire to know each other. They would rather keep going their separate ways; so they finalize it. That's not God's best.

When a husband and wife go separate ways, they cause a breach in the spirit. Eventually, that breach becomes so wide that they are no longer one in spirit. Some are not even aware of each other. I've seen families like that. They go everywhere in separate cars. One says, "I have to do something first; I'll meet you there." Some of those things could wait. If your husband needs you by his side, then get ready and go.

Sometimes that's hard, especially in homes where the wife comes into a knowledge of the Word of God and receives the infilling of the Holy Spirit before the husband. She wants to put herself above her husband. She says, ''I know the Word. That's why everything works out in my life.''

The husband sees the wife as so perfect that he can never attain to the picture she paints. That's the reason many don't come into a fuller knowledge sooner.

The Bible says the unbelieving husband can be won over by the wife's manner of conversation—that is, her manner of living. (1 Peter 3:1.) Just because you're Spirit-filled doesn't make you better than your mate. If you loved him before you came into a fuller knowledge of the Word, you surely should love him afterwards. In fact, the love of God should be even more dominant within you.

It's obvious that some wives are thinking, ''I wish my husband and I were on the same spiritual level. Then we could do things together and everything would be okay.'' If they keep that attitude, they will always find something wrong, even when their husbands do come into a fuller knowledge of the Word.

Let the love of God operate through you. True, sometimes we have to put up with things that we don't appreciate. But because of the love of God, we can put up with these things in order to win over our husbands.

I know—I've been there. My husband and I were just kids when we were married. He knew the Lord, but he had been disillusioned. He didn't understand the drawing of the Spirit of God upon his life because he didn't know the Word, so he was very carnal.

23

I had been brought up in a Christian home, so I knew more of the Word than he did. I knew how to pray. But I was human and I had faults also.

We tend to look at another person's faults; and because they are not in fellowship with God as they should be, we think they are worse than we are. But that's silly, isn't it? Instead, if we will keep working on ourselves, praying, and doing what we know to do, we will win them over faster because we are walking according to the Word. We will be walking the love walk.

Our husbands will see that we are no different in the natural. We still get up and cook their breakfast, get them off to work, and clean the house. We still take care of the home as we always did, because that is our first priority. Everything is in perspective, so we always have the time we desire for the Father God.

It's wrong to do things the other way around—to get so caught up in learning God's Word that we neglect our husbands.

Some women say, "There's a Bible study here on Monday, a blessing service over there Tuesday night, a regular service Wednesday, on Thursday Brother So-and-so is in town, and a seminar starts Friday." They are gone somewhere every night, then wonder why their husbands get mad at them. They are not performing as a wife, but as a spiritual hobo.

The Bible does not tell us to run here and there to fulfill ourselves spiritually. The Word says we must continue to do what we know to do, but that does not come at the expense of our families.

So let's make sure we are seeking God first by tending to our families, and these other things will be added unto us.

3

The Virtuous Woman Revealed

Proverbs 31 gives us a model of the virtuous woman. By studying this passage of Scripture, we can learn how to make ourselves virtuous.

It begins with Proverbs 31:10:

> A capable, intelligent and virtuous woman, who is he who can find her? She is far more precious than jewels, and her value is far above rubies or pearls.
>
> The heart of her husband trusts in her confidently and relies on and believes in her safely, so that he has no lack of honest gain or need of dishonest spoil.
>
> She will comfort, encourage and do him only good as long as there is life within her. (That's our job—assisting, aiding, encouraging, and comforting.)
>
> She seeks out the wool and flax and works with willing hands to develop it.
>
> Proverbs 31:10-13 AMP

Let's look at verse 13 for a moment. The virtuous woman is careful to see that her family has the things they need and that they look nice.

How many times have you seen people adopt an "I don't care" attitude because they are not as prosperous as those around them? They say, "Everybody knows I don't have much, so why should I try to look neat and clean?"

I don't care what level you are on, you can look neat and clean. You can have the best for that level. You can take care of your clothes by laundering them properly and ironing them. You can take care of your shoes and accessories.

If your husband does not know how to coordinate things, help him. If he puts on a wrong combination, just tell him sweetly, "Honey, I don't think that tie goes with that suit—another one might look better." You don't have to say, "That tie looks horrible."

The same rule applies to your children. Show an interest in them. Tell them they should want to look nice because they are children of the King. Some parents think, "Oh well, he's just a kid. Who cares?" He may be "just a kid," but he has feelings too.

Besides having pride in your looks, you should have pride in your home so you can be an effective witness. There should not be toys scattered over the living room floor, or cracker crumbs from where little Johnny has crawled around eating, or the smell of dirty diapers from a full hamper. If someone visits your home, you should dress in more than just a ragged pair of blue jeans and an old shirt. That won't witness to anyone!

Proverbs 31:14 AMP goes on to tell us the virtuous woman "...is like the merchant ships loaded with foodstuffs, she brings her household's food from a far [country]." That simply means she sees that her family has the best. She sees that they are nourished properly by serving balanced meals. She makes sure they are cared for like they should be. No matter how much you believe God for the healing of a child, he will not begin to mend until you have done all you can do in the natural. Proper care is important.

Verse 15 AMP says, "She rises while yet it is night and gets spiritual food for her household and assigns her maids their tasks." Spiritual food is intercession. Just because the man is the head of the house does not mean you as the wife don't have responsibility in that area—you do. You have a responsibility to intercede for him and for your children. Pray and thank the Father that you have His wisdom in every situation. Thank Him that you will say and do the right things, no matter what situation may arise. Thank Him that you speak forth the Word.

In verse 16 AMP we are told, "She considers a new field before she buys or accepts it—expanding prudently [and not courting neglect of her present duties by assuming others]. With her savings [of time and strength] she plants fruitful vines in her vineyard." This scripture could apply to women who work. Some work because they have to; some because they enjoy it. That's fine, as long as you don't neglect the duties you have already assumed as wife and mother. You can always find another job, but you may not always find a peaceful and pleasant home life. Seek God to know exactly what you can handle so that the pressures on you do not become too great.

Verse 17 AMP says, "She girds herself with strength [spiritual, mental and physical fitness for her God-given task] and makes her arms strong and firm." This simply means that in every area—spirit, soul, and body—you are fit to do your job—and that you stay that way.

We are told in verse 18 AMP, "She tastes and sees that her gain from work [with and for God] is good; her lamp goes not out; but it burns on continually through the night [of trouble, privation or sorrow, warning away fear, doubt and distrust]." To me, this simply means you have trained your spirit to be alert to the problems that may arise. Thoughts of fear, doubt, and distrust will arise in your mind. If you are not doing all your part, you will begin to wonder if your husband is doing all his part. That's when the battles begin. Keep yourself strong in the Lord. Make yourself suitable, adaptable, and completing to your husband. Then when these thoughts suddenly come into your mind, you will be able to cast them down immediately.

Verses 19 and 20 tell us:

> She lays her hands to the spindle, and her hands hold the distaff.
>
> She opens her hand to the poor; yes, she reaches out her filled hands to the needy [whether in body, mind or spirit].
> Proverbs 31:19,20 AMP

If your neighbor needs help, you should be ready to help wherever you are needed. The world says, "Don't get involved." But you had better get involved. As a Christian you are a love person, and love never fails. (It also protects, so you won't get hurt.) Because you are an overcomer, love will draw people to you, and you can help them to become overcomers.

Verse 21 AMP says, "She fears not the snow for her family, for all her household are doubly clothed in scarlet." The virtuous woman has no worry about the winter, because she knows her children will have the proper clothing to keep them warm in any situation.

Many times people in northern climates get caught in snowstorms and are unable to get food and other necessities. People panic because they're not prepared. But you don't have to fear these kinds of situations if you are doing what you know to do. If you are functioning as the wife you are to be—relying on Jesus—your household will have double of everything it needs.

Verse 22 AMP tells us, "She makes for herself coverlets, cushions and rugs of tapestry. Her clothing is of linen, pure white and fine, and of purple [such as that of which the clothing of the priests and the hallowed cloths of the temple are made]." The virtuous woman understands prosperity. She realizes that if she is diligent and frugal, her home will have the finest.

Just ask the Father, "Give me wisdom to have my home the way I desire it to be; I want a home that's 'homey.' "

One time the Lord led me to a bedroom suite that was exactly what I wanted—and it was half price! I had asked Him for all-wood furniture that I could afford on my budget. Many times we think, "First I have to find what I want; then when I find it, I'll ask the Father if I can have it." But that's backwards. Go to Him first, and He'll lead you to it!

By doing what the Lord tells you to do, blessings will come to you in abundance. But when those blessings begin, remember where they came from! The first fruit belongs to the Lord. Don't be stingy with your money and try to hold onto it. Many begin to trust the Lord; but when they get blessed, they begin to get stingy. They have a continual struggle, because things have become their security. There is only one source of security—God. Everything on this earth is temporary. If your security is in things, you are on shaky ground.

Verse 23 AMP says, "Her husband is known in the city's gates, when he sits among the elders of the land." He is known because she has done her part to see that he has a happy home. She has interceded for him as he learned how to exercise the wisdom of God. As a result he has begun to be successful in every area of life.

Verses 24 through 31 AMP complete for us the picture of the virtuous woman:

> She makes fine linen garments and leads others to buy them; she delivers to the merchants girdles [or sashes that free one for service].

29

Strength and dignity are her clothing and her position is strong and secure. She rejoices over the future—the latter day or time to come [knowing that she and her family are in readiness for it]!

She opens her mouth with skillful and godly Wisdom, and in her tongue is the law of kindness—giving counsel and instruction.

She looks well to how things go in her household, and the bread of idleness [gossip, discontent and self-pity] she will not eat.

Her children rise up and call her blessed [happy, fortunate and to be envied]; and her husband boasts of and praises her, saying,

Many daughters have done virtuously, nobly and well [with the strength of character that is steadfast in goodness] but you excel them all.

Charm and grace are deceptive, and beauty is vain [because it is not lasting], but a woman who reverently and worshipfully fears the Lord, she shall be praised!

Give her of the fruit of her hands, and let her own works praise her in the gates of the city!

Wasn't Jesus known for His works? And here on this earth we are His light shining forth. We must do what is at hand, caring for our husbands and children. Then the praise comes. Your husband will be proud to say, "This is my wife." Your children will be proud to say, "This is my mother." Then you can turn and give all the glory to God, because He made you a virtuous woman.

PART II
The Role of the
Christian Wife

4

Guidelines To Perfect
Us As Godly Wives

First Peter 3:1-6 deals with a subject which women sometimes don't like: submission. However, we all need to face it. Learn to be honest with yourself, because in honesty there is joy. You know exactly where you stand and what areas in your life need improvement.

Many times we get caught up in vain thinking. We wonder, "What would my husband do without me?" But what would you do without him? You were made for him.

Let's read 1 Peter 3:1-6 *AMP* together:

> In like manner you married women, be submissive to your own husbands—subordinate yourselves as being secondary to and dependent on them, and adapt yourselves to them. So that even if any do not obey the Word [of God], they may be won over not by discussion but by the [godly] lives of their wives,
>
> When they observe the pure and modest way in which you conduct yourselves, together with your reverence [for your husband. That is, you are to feel for him all that reverence includes]—to respect, defer to, revere him; [revere means] to honor, esteem (appreciate, prize), and [in the human sense] adore him; [and adore means] to admire, praise, be devoted to, deeply love and enjoy [your husband].
>
> Let not yours be the [merely] external adorning with [elaborate] interweaving and knotting of the hair, the wearing of jewelry, or changes of clothes;
>
> But let it be the inward adorning and beauty of the hidden person of the heart, with the incorruptible and unfading charm of a gentle and peaceful spirit, which (is not

anxious or wrought up, but) is very precious in the sight of God.

For it was thus that the pious women of old who hoped in God were (accustomed) to beautify themselves, and were submissive to their husbands—adapting themselves to them as themselves secondary and dependent upon them.

It was thus that Sarah obeyed Abraham (following his guidance and acknowledging his headship over her by) calling him lord—master, leader, authority. And you are now her true daughters if you do right and let nothing terrify you—not giving way to hysterical fears or letting anxieties unnerve you.

Notice the first verse talks about winning your husband by your godly life. This verse can be adapted to every woman—those who are married and those who have friends whose husbands are not in the Word. Just as the wife is to live a godly life, you as a Christian friend must do the same. You do not have to submit yourself to your friend's husband, but you can let the Spirit of God rise up within you so you don't influence your friend the wrong way.

I have seen unmarried women talk negatively to married friends about their husbands. They say, "It's not your fault these things are happening in your marriage. After all, you have the Word in you. Spiritually, you are high above him."

Be careful to always be a proper influence. You may not be a wife any longer, but you're still a woman, and you still have the responsibility of seeing that the character of God flows from you. Don't be a stumbling block to others. Take this scripture for yourself, and be the woman God intends you to be by your manner of living.

Another thing—be careful not to present yourself as having greater knowledge than your husband. This is difficult for a man's ego. You may say, "He shouldn't have an ego." But God gave it to him so he should have it.

Many women do come into a fuller knowledge of the Word that changes their lives. They grow and mature. But if they get so taken up with learning that they think only of themselves, they move over into the selfish realm. They can no longer protect their husband from attacks of the enemy.

You are to surround him with protection. You do that by your manner of living and by how you treat him. Without that protection your husband is more open to the enemy's maneuvers against him.

Even if you are born again and your husband is not, your marriage relationship should not change. There should simply be placed within you a stronger desire to love him and surround him with prayer and the God kind of love. He will be able to see that a change has come in your life, but that you still love him.

If you can't do that, then the love of God is not operating in your life. The Bible says God gave His only Son—the best He had. (John 3:16.) God accepts everybody just as they are in their unlovely state. If we are like Him, we have to do the same.

Be sure to conduct yourself in a pure and modest way.

Let's say you have influenced your husband enough that he has decided to come to church. In our circles of Christian fellowship, we let the love of God flow. But your husband may not be a new creation; and if not, his mind is not renewed to the Word of God. Be careful about hugging all your brothers in the Lord. Your husband won't understand that. He still thinks like the world thinks. Immediately the devil will come to him and say, "The reason your wife likes this so well is because they have all this free love here. The women can go around and hug all the men as long as they do it 'in the Name of Jesus Christ.' "

I've counseled women whose husbands have felt this way. The wives always ask, "What can I do to change things?" And my answer is always the same: be modest and pure in your conduct. This does not mean you have to put yourself in bondage, but be careful. If you keep yourself in the presence of the Lord at all times and confess His wisdom, you will act accordingly.

Also, no matter what kind of spiritual change you have had, continue to reverence your husband. Because you have found the truth, you should honor and respect your husband even more.

This is where some women get hung up. They say, "How can I defer to my husband when I know he's not right?" There is a fine line here. Is he "not right" because you think you're above him spiritually? Do you feel his ideas are silly because he's not mature in the Lord? Or, does he want you to do something that goes against a conviction in your heart because of your relationship with your Father God? You must decide.

Another thing we are to do according to the Word of God is adore our husbands. I've said, "I adore my husband," then had women say, "But you're only supposed to adore God."

The Word does tell us to adore God. That's in the spiritual sense. But in the human sense we are to adore our husbands. In adoring them, we learn to praise, respect, and be devoted to them. In the human sense our husbands are to be first place in our lives.

We are also to enjoy our husbands. To enjoy means "to take pleasure and satisfaction in; to have for one's use or benefit." Take pleasure and satisfaction in your husband. He is there for your use and benefit (not to maneuver, manipulate, or take advantage of).

5

A Bible Outline
For Marital Relations

The Scriptures are very clear in providing a picture of the marriage relationship. First Corinthians 7:4 AMP says, "For the wife does not have [exclusive] authority and control over her own body, but the husband [has his rights]; likewise also the husband does not have [exclusive] authority and control over his body, but the wife [has her rights]."

You are to take pleasure in your husband. Each of you is to be a delight to the other—spirit, soul, and body.

The following verse, 1 Corinthians 7:5 AMP, tells us: "Do not refuse and deprive and defraud each other (of your due marital rights), except perhaps by mutual consent for a time, that you may devote yourselves unhindered to prayer. But afterwards resume marital relations, lest Satan tempt you [to sin] through your lack of restraint of sexual desire."

The Scriptures are saying you do not have full authority and control over your body, but neither does your husband have authority and control over his. Give to one another. Because you become one—spirit, soul, and body—with your husband, you should treat his body as your own. This means not abusing, taking advantage of, or drawing away from each other in the marital relationship.

This is a difficult area for some women. If you are refusing, depriving, and defrauding, then your thinking is like the world and not like the Bible. Your thinking is what man, through traditional religion, has put on you.

You are to enjoy your husband. *Enjoyment* means "taking pleasure and satisfaction in." You and he are for each other's use and benefit. It's important that you learn this concerning sex between husband and wife.

People are having problems in this area. Most times it is caused by the woman being too cold. She does not enjoy herself in the bedroom and, as a result, tension is created in the husband. He feels that he can't satisfy her because of her actions and reactions, so he tends to draw away.

But because you—the woman—were made for the man, you must adapt yourself and make yourself suitable and completing to your husband. When the Bible says you are to enjoy your husband, that's what it means!

In the generation before mine, "sex" was a dirty word. That was because Satan had perverted it. Christians looked at the perversion and not at the good.

In the bedroom, the sexual relationship between you and your husband is a gift from God. He wants the two of you to be one in body, fulfilled.

Women have said to me, "I just can't give vent to how I feel; I would be so embarrassed." But why should you be embarrassed? The two of you are one. Your husband desires you to give vent to your feelings. Then he will know that you enjoy him as much as he enjoys you. He needs to know that you love him dearly and that he is first in your life from the human standpoint. When you give of yourself fully and completely to him, then not only is he satisfied, but you are too.

There are so many frustrated women, especially in religious circles, because they don't understand this. They are frustrated because they do not let the true love of God flow through them in their sexual relations. But God says we are supposed to do that. We're not supposed to refuse, deprive, and defraud each other. So, ladies, the headache is no excuse! You'll forget all about your headache if you do as you're supposed to and be the wife God intended you to be.

Get before the Father God and let Him show you how you are to respond. According to the Word of God, the only time you and your husband can refuse each other is to devote yourselves unhindered to prayer. And this has to be done only by mutual agreement.

These are areas we sometimes have to work at. But we should. God made us woman, and He made us for man in the natural sense. He gave us everything we need to make ourselves suitable, adaptable, and completing. Because we are joined first with our husband in the spirit realm, then it is a beautiful time in the physical realm. The union is complete.

Sexual relations are to the marriage as food is to the body. Without food you die. Without sexual relations in a marriage union, death will come. It doesn't happen all at once. Just like when you quit eating food, you don't die the first day; it takes a while. But eventually you reach the point of death, then there's no feeling. If that happens in your marriage, then your spiritual life is hindered. You are not walking totally in the will of God and how He made you as a woman.

In this day and age, sex is just a household word in the world's eyes. First, it was something you didn't talk about. Now that's all some people talk about. They flaunt it, but in the perverted sense.

You have to view sex as something pure and wonderful, holy before the Lord. To Him it's a beautiful union. He made it that way, and we should see it that way because we don't want death to come. The sexual relationship in your marriage is part of the life-giving process in the natural. Whether or not you have children, it is still part of the life-giving process.

Noted speaker Dick Mills has a teaching called "Hearts and Flowers." In that teaching, he explains how a man needs to have an understanding of the different things a woman goes through in her menstrual cycle. He also explains about a man's ego—how it is of God, and how the woman is to feed it. He says that a man has reached his highest point of ego (scientists have proved this) when a woman gives herself to him and he has reached a fulfilled, completed climax. Why is this? Because the life process God has given him for the natural has joined with the woman who was made for him. They have become one naturally (or physically), completely fulfilled in that area.

Many want to think little or nothing about the sexual union. Some women teach their children that sex is something to be endured, like cleaning house or giving the children a bath.

But God made you a woman, skillfully and carefully handcrafted to be desired and admired. You have to fulfill that role. If you don't (especially if your husband is not in the Word), the lust of the flesh can take over in his life. The marriage union will no longer be pure. He is looking at other women, and it's your fault. That's a big responsibility. But God has given us the ability we need to make ourselves adaptable, suitable, and completing to the one God has given us. We can do it.

Here's something else important. First Corinthians 7:14 AMP says, ''For the unbelieving husband is set apart (separated, withdrawn from heathen contamination and affiliated with the Christian people) by union with his consecrated (set-apart) wife . . . .'' This is another reason you need to keep your marriage union perfect and pure. You are the one who keeps him withdrawn from heathen contamination.

This passage goes on to say that the unbelieving wife is separated through her union with a consecrated husband, and that the children are prepared for God, pure and clean, because of that union.

We, as Christian wives, have a big responsibility, because of our union with God, to maintain and uphold that marriage union to the best of our ability. But God will not call you to do anything he does not give you the equipment and ability to do. He has called you to be woman in this earth. Therefore, you have everything you need in your natural body to be a woman.

6
Meeting Needs In
The Soulish Realm

We have talked about the sexual part of marriage—how to be adaptable and completing in the physical realm. Now I want us to consider the soulish realm. We are to be suitable, adapting, and completing in that area as well.

The best way to exercise and accomplish this is through communication. Communication feeds the soul. If we communicate properly, there won't be assumptions in the mind—thoughts like, "I really don't know him as I should."

One way to communicate is to share with your husband what God has shown you in your devotions. Together, you are one, so that which affects you will affect your husband also. Share your feelings. Communicate in everything you are involved in.

That does not mean you are to meet him at the door saying, "You won't believe what happened to me today; I hardly coped with it." That's not communication. It is merely an exercise of your frustration. Communication is being able to talk freely with another person.

Many times a woman can talk more freely to a friend than to her husband. Your husband should be, first of all, your friend—then, your lover. If you don't share communication—feeding the thinking faculty and emotions—then he will not be your friend and your union won't be complete.

41

My husband and I always share the Word together. Many times, though we are studying different subjects, something I share with him will shed light on something he's studying. Therefore, we keep a balance spiritually.

To feed the soulish realm, you need to spend time with your husband to communicate your thoughts and feelings with each other. You will then be able to know one another well. This builds trust. My husband and I are true friends. I know how he will act or react, what he expects, and what is important to him. He knows the same about me.

Sometimes you can get caught up in "faith" and can't talk about your feelings. You think that to do so would be confessing the wrong thing. But if the feelings are already there, they are fact.

If a thought comes to your mind, but you disregard it and put the Word in its place, it's not yet a feeling. However, when things have come against you, and feelings have become a part of you, you had better express them. Then you and your husband can join yourselves together, ask for the wisdom of God, and do something about the situation.

Many times by communicating feelings you are able to see areas where the enemy has deceived you, and you are relieved immediately. You realize that a certain "feeling" was just something the enemy placed in your mind, even though it seemed a part of you.

On the other hand, there are real differences to be worked out between men and women because of our personalities. Yes, men think differently than women. Many times it's hard for us to understand their thinking, but in the same way it's hard for them to understand our thinking. That's another reason communication is so important. It helps us to understand why they think and react the way they do; and they, in turn, begin to understand us. This brings a balance in the soulish realm.

You can have assurance and know that he understands you. You think, "He's not going to condemn me or put me down." Then because you understand him, you won't condemn or put him down. You can love each other and be a friend to one another as you talk and pray together about the situations that arise. You are true friends; and isn't that what friends are for?

Communication, then, is important in every area—spirit, soul, and body. We become a total union with our mate, living in ideal harmony, bound together in the love of God.

God desires this of us, because this is how He made us. He created us so He could have fellowship with us. He wants us to know Him not only as the Creator, but as a friend. He truly cares about us.

That true fellowship and friendship is vital to the marriage union. Sometimes we take that union for granted. The husband gets up in the morning, showers and shaves, combs his hair, puts on his clothes, and eats breakfast. We think it's just a routine thing. But it's not; it's life—a process of giving and receiving. Yet the wife has to give first in order to receive.

You—the woman—were made for man. Now it's not a one-way street; it's not a matter of waiting on him hand and foot. It's seeking the wisdom of God and walking in the ability He gave you. You can walk in wisdom. Proverbs 3:17 AMP, speaking about wisdom, says, "Her ways are highways of pleasantness, and all her paths are peace." If you don't have that peace and pleasantness, you're not walking in the full wisdom of God.

Sometimes today we emphasize the Word so much that we don't have the prayer time with the Lord that we should. It is important to know the Word, but no less important is time of conversation with the Lord. Prayer is not telling God all your problems—prayer is communication. Prayer is your speaking forth the Word to God, and His responding to it. That builds a confidence in you that He will do what He says in His Word.

Sometimes people think, "If I confess this a hundred times, I'll have it." Ridiculous! They are not walking in faith, but in works.

What counts is studying the Word, meditating the Word, and letting it become a part of you. Then as you pray to the Father, communicating to Him, the Spirit of God rises up within you, and understanding comes. That is when you begin to receive revelation knowledge.

So first, we must communicate with our Creator. Secondly, we must communicate with the one God has given us. Remember, we were created for him—not he for us.

PART III
The Role of the
Christian Mother

7

. . . From the Womb

We have dealt with the subjects of woman and wife. Now let's consider our role as "mother."

Isaiah 44:24 in *The Amplified Bible* tells us something very interesting concerning children. It reads, "Thus says the Lord, your Redeemer, and He Who formed you from the womb: I am the Lord Who made all things . . . ."

I want to center on the phrase, ". . . He Who formed you from the womb . . . ." That means life in the womb is being God-formed.

If you become pregnant, it is important that from the time you are aware of conception to speak the Word to your child.

Speak forth the goodness of God. Speak that the child is alive unto God. Speak that the child is just like its Maker. Speak that the child is healthy, strong, and perfect because it is being formed by God. You are speaking forth truth, and truth will prevail.

We must do this not from the time the child is in our arms, but from the time of its conception. In the natural, we are the child's life-giving source. But in the spiritual, God is forming him, and it is important that we speak what God says. God and His Word are one.

We must start speaking to that life within us, proclaiming it to be perfect and whole. Sometimes we make a mistake and get caught up in the natural, thinking about whether we want a boy or girl, or twins. We forget the basics of speaking the Word about the child being perfect and whole. But if we will speak that, we will always have the knowledge and assurance that our child is perfect. We won't have hassles in our minds when we hear negative things other mothers might say.

Because you put within yourself the knowledge that the life within you is being formed by God, you have spoken His Word over your child. When the baby is delivered, it will be perfect, whole, and complete.

Then from the time you hold the child in your arms, you begin to whisper in its ear, "God is your Creator and your Father. Jesus is the Lord of our home." That child's spirit is alive unto God from the time he is born into this earth.

8

Training Up Your Child

Second Timothy 3:15 AMP talks about training up our children.

> And how from your childhood you have had a knowledge of and been acquainted with the sacred writings which are able to instruct you and give you the understanding for salvation which comes through faith in Christ Jesus [that is, through the leaning of the entire human personality on God in Christ Jesus in absolute trust and confidence in His power, wisdom, and goodness].

As a child, I was trained up like this. I cannot tell you when I received Christ, because I was so young. Yet I remember an awareness of it. I was taught about Christ from the time I was very small. Christianity was a way of life for me. I can remember our home being full of love because God was there. The Word of God was always read, taught, and experienced. And that's the way it should be in your home.

When I became of age, I thought I knew everything. I strayed from that way of life a bit. But I never turned my back on it because it was too real inside me. I knew it was life and truth, and I knew it would work in my life if I would do it.

My husband says I've always been Miss Goody-Two-Shoes. But in my eyes, I was not. I did not live up to the standards I had set for myself. I let people influence me rather than God. Still, I never strayed to the point that I was out in the world. I always would come back to God, renew my fellowship, and go on with Him.

That's how your children can be if you will talk to them about Jesus from the time you hold them in your arms. Tell them Who He is and Who the Father God is and what they have done. Speak the Word.

There are children who have been taught that way from the home into the nursery where they talk and sing songs about Jesus. They know if they get hurt they should pray. That's what being natural is; you're just like your Father God. And that's the way we should begin with our children.

Many times it's difficult for us, as parents, to take the responsibility and use the authority we have. Often it's hard for us as women. We want to leave it to our husbands. But you have just as much a part in it as he does.

A scripture that has helped is Proverbs 8:14 AMP: "I have counsel and sound knowledge, I have understanding, I have might and power." I had to confess this as a mother to build confidence in me that I could discipline my children according to the Word of God. Through confessing that scripture, consistency came. I understood that in my responsibility there was authority and I had to take it. This is how I built my confidence that I could do as I was to do as a parent.

You have a responsibility to teach your children the Word of God, and you must begin when they are small. But it's also important to put within them the principle of discipline. That teaches them to be a disciplined person (not because mommie is disciplined and wants them to be the same, but because it will make them a better person).

Because of my nature, it was hard for me to stand in the authority that was mine. I found it easier to love the children and let them go. But if you do not discipline your children, you do not love them.

Cultivating discipline in your child will cause him to understand authority and have respect for you, for himself, and for the people and things around him.

Proverbs 19:18 *AMP* says, "Discipline your son while there is hope, but do not [indulge your angry resentments by undue chastisements and] set yourself to his ruin." There is a proper way to discipline—not through anger, but through love. Because you love your child you want to keep him from error. You want to show him what is wrong in his life and teach him how to be a loving and obedient child.

Another scripture on discipline is Ephesians 6:4 *AMP*: "Fathers, do not irritate and provoke your children to anger—do not exasperate them to resentment—but rear them [tenderly] in the training and discipline and the counsel and admonition of the Lord."

That shows us we are not to discipline our children in a fit of anger. We are to calm ourselves and let the love that is within us flow forth. In a fit of anger you might discipline your child wrongly. Sometimes when you are frustrated, any little thing the child does will trigger anger. The child may have done a small thing that may not require a spanking, but only a word of understanding or wisdom. Disciplining in anger will bring fear. Keep doing that, and it will cause resentment and eventually lead to your ruin.

The way a child turns out reflects on the parents. So make sure that you are walking in love. Speak to your children calmly and discipline them calmly. Whether the situation requires a spanking or just a word of understanding, do it in love with the Word of God. Then your child will understand your motives and reasonings.

My father never disciplined us without sitting down with us and saying, "Do you understand why you are being punished?" He would make us tell what we had done and why we were being disciplined. If we didn't know, then he would explain. But he still punished us.

We understood that our parents were the authority, and we respected them. We understood that they loved us and disciplined us because of that. We understood that the punishment was for our benefit. Because they were much older than we, they knew more about life and could give us knowledge, understanding, and wisdom.

One thing to remember when talking to your children is don't get so carried away with your explanation that you never get around to a spanking. Children are smart. They learn, "If mommie thinks I don't understand, she'll sit down and start talking about it, and I'll never get the punishment." They know how to manipulate and maneuver their parents (especially mommie, because she's with them more).

This is why we need to confess that we have knowledge, wisdom, and understanding in these areas.

Another Scripture passage that teaches on this subject is Proverbs 10:12,13 AMP:

> **Hatred stirs up contentions, but love covers all transgressions.**
>
> **In the lips of him who has discernment, skillful and godly Wisdom is found, but discipline and the rod are for the back of him who is without sense and understanding.**

No one could say it better than that. Notice the scripture says there is a proper place for the rod—the back of the child.

When I was little, I would visit a certain relative. It always unnerved me to be at her house when any of her children got into trouble. She would yell, scream, and hit any part of the child's body which happened to be next to her. It always upset me, and though I wasn't involved, I always cried. I was always disciplined in love. Her kind of discipline frightened me. It didn't seem to be in love.

My dad made us lie across the bed when he spanked us. I hated that, so I learned quickly. But it seemed that my brother was always in trouble. I would run to my room, shut the door, and cry because I felt sorry for him. Yet I knew he deserved it.

When my mother disciplined us, she always said, "I'm doing this because I love you." I thought, "Oh, sure you are." But because my parents gave me the Word, there came a time when I did understand.

So remember to always give your child the reason for what you're doing.

Another good scripture on discipline is Proverbs 13:24 *AMP*: "He who spares his rod [of discipline] hates his son, but he who loves him diligently disciplines and punishes him early." The word *diligently* means consistently.

Don't keep saying, "Johnny, if you do that again, I'm going to spank you." Eventually, Johnny will realize he can do it as long as he wants because you don't mean what you say. Then when Johnny's behavior totally irritates you, you react in complete anger. All that does is build fear and resentment in the child. You are not being diligent and disciplining in love.

There have been times when I would wait to deal with a situation until I could calmly discipline them. One Sunday morning as we were ready to leave for church, one of my children was disobedient. Because of the lack of time, I said, "I'll deal with you later, when I'm calm and you've thought about it a while."

We went to church, ate lunch, and were on our way home when that child said, "Mommie, I've thought about it. Are you calm?" My children wanted to get it over with because they knew I never forgot it. They knew if I loved them I would do exactly what I said.

Some people thought my husband and I were too strict about making our children mind. But we did it so the principles of God could be formed in them.

When they were small (and babies do have tempers), they knew by the tone of my voice that I meant "hush," so they hushed. By the time they were five and six months old they got their little hands and legs spanked. They understood what "no" meant and what a spat on the leg meant. I was not abusing them. They didn't even have a red mark, but they knew what I meant.

I can remember an incident concerning my middle child, Cookie. She was about seven months old. We were at my cousin's house, and she kept crawling around the stereo. On either side of the stereo was a rack for records. She kept trying to pull those out. I would look at her and say, "No." She'd move her hand, crawl away, then look up and grin as if to say, "Oh, I'm so sweet, Mommie." And that is what you think—they're precious. But they won't be precious long if you don't discipline them.

She did that about five or six times, and each time I spanked her hand and said, "No." After a while she got the message, crawled off, and found the toys she was supposed to be playing with.

Many people would say, "Well, she's just a baby. Pick up the records and put them where she can't reach them." But that's not teaching your child properly. When you go to another house where the records aren't put away, you'll be embarrassed.

Another excellent scripture passage is Proverbs 23:12-14 AMP:

> Apply your mind to instruction and correction, and your ears to the words of knowledge.
>
> Withhold not discipline from the child, for if you strike and punish him with the [reed-like] rod, he will not die.
>
> You shall whip him with the rod and deliver his life from Sheol [Hades, the place of the dead].

You have seen the result in this country of letting children "do their thing." They did their thing all over college campuses—destruction and death. This happened because they had not been disciplined when they were wrong. They had no respect for anyone or anything. And they did not understand authority. Many times this led to destruction for others, and for themselves.

The responsibility for how your children turn out rests on your shoulders, parents. God created you to have children, so He has given you all the knowledge and ability you need. But it's up to you to exercise it. The Scriptures tell us not to spare the rod.

God disciplines us through His Word. It is gentle, simple, and kind; but it penetrates and we know that we have been chastised. Yet He always does it lovingly.

That's how we should be with our children. They know when they have been chastised. But because it's been done in love and with a soft voice, they understand it's for their good; so they change their behavior.

We need to show them this spiritual and natural parallel. That's how you build into them the principle of morality. They learn that you're somebody and they're somebody. They understand that we must be good stewards and care for the things we have.

As I was sharing this with a lady one time, she said, "Are you serious about what you're saying?"

I said, "Of course I am; I've given you scriptures and it's the Word of God."

"Well, no wonder I don't have anything."

I had never been to her home, so I said, "What do you mean?"

She answered, "My husband has worked hard. We have a nice home, but our furniture and carpets are in shambles because I let my kids run through the house with food. They jump on the furniture and play everywhere. I never thought anything about it, because that's how I was raised. But isn't it terrible that my house is always in shambles because I'm in ignorance?''

That's how the devil would like people to think. Eventually, in that kind of environment division will come. Satan can tear that home apart. So you need to teach your children to be obedient, to care for their bodies, their clothes, their toys, and the furniture.

If my children ever had something to eat or drink, they sat at the kitchen table. Some people thought I was really cruel. But that's the way my parents raised me, and it didn't cause me to be in rebellion.

Teach your children that the couch is to sit on—not to stand on. The bed is to lie on—not to jump on. If they want to jump, send them outside.

You can learn to believe God for things; but before you reach that point, you have to work hard for those things. Your children need to understand this. That's why so many young people in this day and age think the world owes them a living. They have not learned responsibility.

You must teach them that they have within them the ability to be successful, thoughtful, and respectful of other people's property.

My mother would never let us leave the house without making sure our outfits were clean, matched, and put together properly. When we would go to some ministers' houses, it amazed me how their children looked. Their clothes were dirty. They might have one shoe on with a sock, and the other without. Their hair might look like it hadn't been combed all day. We didn't have a lot when I was little, but we were taught to be clean and neat. We looked nice and took pride in our appearance.

Sometimes when we were going out to lunch with people, my mother would say to the other parent, ''Can I help get your children ready to go?'' That parent would answer, "There's bologna in the refrigerator; they can fix a sandwich when they get hungry. We don't take them out because they don't act like your children."

I felt sorry for those children. It was a treat for me to go out with my parents, because at that time we didn't go out to eat very often. They took pride in my knowing how to behave myself. I knew when to talk and when to be quiet. I knew when to sit still, and I knew when they said, "Be still," they meant it. I wasn't fearful of that. I just understood that they were the authority and I respected them for it.

One other thing...some ministers acted as if the people in their church were more important than their children. As a result, the children resented those people and had no respect for their parents. Many ended up as alcoholics and some were killed because of drunken driving by the time they were twenty years old.

I have heard those parents say to my folks, "What did we do wrong? Look at your children. They're serving God. They understand authority. They have respect for themselves and others."

When a parent has just lost a child, it's the wrong time to tell them what they've done wrong. You have to speak in love and share with them what you have done as a parent. They do get the message then, but it's too late. That's why the Bible says to be diligent about disciplining your children while they are young. Don't wait until your child is 13 or 14 years old to make them mind. It will be too late.

Your children need true love and understanding. The only way to give them that love and understanding is to give them God's Word. First, you as a parent must become established in the Word; then you must discipline your children according to what the Word says.

Here's another scripture that applies to raising children: "A gentle tongue [with its healing power] is a tree of life, but willful contrariness in it breaks down the spirit" (Prov. 15:4 AMP).

The way parents talk to their children is vital to their upbringing. Harsh words can eventually cause a child's will to be broken. Many times those children are scarred for life. Unless they get in the Word of God and allow the Holy Spirit to work in them, they will never overcome some of those scars and hurts.

God desires that you be gentle with your children, not only in your mannerisms, but with your tongue. Sometimes there is nothing wrong with the actual words spoken to our children, but the tone of our voice is improper and can cause a negative effect. The Bible never speaks of breaking a child's spirit or will. It speaks of molding it according to the Word. That will is what the child has to work with, because he will use is to choose the way of the Word or the way of the world.

Many children whose wills have been broken end up in mental institutions. Psychiatrists try to rebuild in them what has been destroyed; but without the Word and its healing power, that restoration will never be done.

So, parent, be careful to discipline in love and with a gentle tongue. But, nevertheless, discipline; and remember to explain the situation to your child. He must have an understanding of what he is being disciplined for.

Many times it seems the responsibility of discipline rests more on the mother than the father because she is with the child more. But that's not true. Communicate with your husband so that you know how he feels about discipline. Then the two of you will be in unity. Because of that agreement, you can enforce the discipline you both have decided upon. You don't need to tell the child, "Wait until your daddy gets home...."

Also, you must never correct your husband while he is disciplining your children. No matter if he's right or wrong, don't do it. That child will see that he can manipulate mom against dad to get what he wants.

I've seen fathers discipline children. But as soon as daddy was gone, mommie had baby in her lap loving him and saying, "That mean old daddy." Instead of teaching that child the way of the Word, she was leading him down the path of destruction.

If you don't agree with the way your husband has disciplined, wait and discuss it calmly later when the child is not in your presence.

Another thing—don't be ashamed to ask your child's forgivenss if you have disciplined him incorrectly. You are the example. By doing that, you are teaching him forgiveness. Be big enough to say to your child, "I'm sorry. I didn't discipline you correctly. You must forgive me." When you do that, a strong bond is formed. They understand that you do love them and have a desire to discipline them by the Word. I've done that with my children. It wasn't hard because my heart was right before God, and I wanted everything to be right in my household.

Don't let those things slip by. Don't think, "Oh well, he's just a child; he doesn't know." Children are very sensitive. They do know. So check up on yourself to make sure you are walking in love and disciplining according to the Word.

Show your children Ephesians 6:1 AMP which says: "Children, obey your parents in the Lord [as His representatives], for this is just and right." The second verse continues, "Honor (esteem and value as precious) your father and your mother; this is the first commandment with a promise." We need to imprint this on our children's spirits.

As children, my brother and I knew that by heart. Dad always used to ask, "Do you know what the first commandment with promise is?" We always responded, "Yes, we know what it is." And he always said, "Tell me what it is." That built within us understanding, respect, and character.

That's how you need to treat your children. Don't have the attitude, "I don't have time." You'd better take time, unless you want a lot of heartache and disappointment, seeing your children suffer when it isn't necessary.

Many times children suffer because their parents didn't have time to build character into them. They were too busy with their own lives. That is not the way of the Word.

I'm not telling you anything new. But you need to stir yourself up. Make sure you are doing everything you know to do.

Are you being consistent?

Are you walking in the fullness of what you know?

Are you molding that child with the character of God?

Are you being a good example? No matter what you say to your children, they are going to follow your example—whether good or bad. Make your actions line up with your words. Don't tell them, "Do as I say, not as I do."

Remember, Proverbs 22:6 AMP: "Train up a child in the way he should go [and in keeping with his individual gift or bent], and when he is old he will not depart from it."

Notice it says, "in keeping with his individual gift." Each child has a gift within him that will cause him to excel in life. My son is very creative; but that gift must be channeled by discipline, love, understanding, and knowledge.

By disciplining our children correctly, we not only develop a parent-child relationship, but a friendship as well.

One of the greatest pleasures I ever had came as a result of this kind of friendship. My youngest daughter and her husband used to live in Johannesburg, South Africa. On her twenty-first birthday she sent me a dozen red roses and a note: "Mom, I love you, and because of you I have had a full, beautiful twenty-one years."

Times like this give parents their reward on the earth. The Scriptures describe it clearly. Proverbs 31:28 AMP says, "Her children rise up and call her blessed."

9

Practical Relations
In Home Living

We have talked about discipline and how the children reflect back on the parents. Proverbs 20:11 *AMP* says, "Even a child is known by his acts, whether or not what he does is pure and right." So many times we see a child act up in public and think, "Well, I know how he's disciplined at home!" The home life, then, is revealed by the child's behavior.

As I mentioned earlier, people used to say my husband and I were too strict with our girls when they were young. They were only nineteen months apart, and we were very young when we had them. Also, during the first few years of our marriage Buddy was out of fellowship with the Lord, and we were not living for God like we should have been.

Many situations arose in which I didn't know what to do, so I would look to the Holy Spirit, our Comforter, and would intercede for Buddy and our home. That was all I knew to do. If you find yourself feeling the same way, pray in the Spirit and confess the wisdom of God. Say, "I'm a child of God and I have the Holy Spirit. I know when I pray in the Spirit I'm praying the perfect prayer. Therefore, the Holy Spirit is at work in my home. I confess His wisdom so I will know what to do and when to do it; I will know what to say and what not to say. I will work along with my husband, and we will be united in every area of our life together."

Confess these things. They are part of the Word. If you don't confess them, they will not work in your home. Your household will continually be in strife and upheaval.

Remember, you can always rely on the Holy Spirit and begin to pray. Sometimes during the day a thought will come to you about your child. Most people think, "Oh, that's just me; I'm a protective mother." But many times it is the Holy Spirit prompting you to intercede. Perhaps the child is having a problem in school.

Did you know that in some schools there are evil spirits coming against children who know the Lord? Many times when my girls would come home from school, I would know when they walked through the door that a spirit had been harassing them.

You have to take authority over the spirit and say, "You don't belong in my home, and you have no right to harass my child. This home belongs to the Father God, and in the Name of Jesus you cannot stay here."

Use your everyday authority. That is a simple way to say it, but it's the truth.

So many times we think our child's behavior is "only a phase." There are phases every child must go through, but you don't have to put up with one disaster after another! There can also be uplifting times to help the child understand what is going on. Sit down with him, read the scripture that pertains to the situation, then take authority over the problem.

If a child is small, perhaps in elementary school, you can take authority over spirits without the child even knowing it, and thus eliminate fear. You can take him in your arms, love him, and say, "In the Name of Jesus, Father, I thank You for my child who has peace, love, and joy."

We have talked about training up your children in the way they should go. Remember too that while training them in the way of the Word and taking authority over spirits, we must also keep our confession right.

Many parents say, "I taught my children about the Lord when they were very young, but look at them now. They're not living for the Lord." Their confession about their children is keeping them from coming any closer to living for the Lord.

My husband lived the first few years of his life with his grandfather, who was a Pentecostal minister. They would have daily devotions, share the Word, and pray together. When a situation would arise, the Word was quoted, so Buddy got full of the Word as a child.

Then when he went back to live with his father, the atmosphere was different. His father had quit living for the Lord and had gone the way of the world. Buddy tried to go that way too, but the Word in him was too great. He was continually drawn back to it. He was never happy trying to follow his father, because the Word was imbedded in his spirit.

As a parent, continually share the Word with your children. Then say, "Father, I did as Your Word said. I trained up my child in the way he should go. He knows the Word and it is in his spirit."

If it seems that he is straying from the Word in his later years, you can add, "Even though the Word is lying dormant in his spirit, it is there; and I know in the Name of Jesus that he will awaken and follow after it." Remember, the Word works, and no matter how the circumstances may seem, your child will follow after what he has been taught. Don't look at circumstances. Say, "Lord, I did as the Word says. Therefore, it is so and it is done." That way you will keep a calmness and strength within you.

If we have disciplined and trained our children properly, we must not be overly self-conscious about their behavior if it is not always perfect. I had this problem concerning my children. Maybe it stemmed from my past—people expecting me to be prim and proper because I was the minister's daughter.

With that kind of attitude, you have a tendency to withdraw and hold your child to yourself, not letting anybody see how he acts. I got to the point of almost being physically sick over this. I had to say, "Lord, forgive me; I am wrong."

Children are children and kids are kids. No matter what you teach them, they are going to do and say things you don't want.

Here is a scripture you can read to your children to show them what makes their parents happy:

> **The father of the [uncompromisingly] righteous—the upright, in right standing with God—shall greatly rejoice, and he who becomes the father of a wise child shall have joy in him.**
>
> **Let your father and your mother be glad, and let her who bore you rejoice.**
>
> **Proverbs 23:24,25 AMP**

When children see that they are doing what the Word says, and that the Word works, they will have a desire to do those things. Fear won't be involved. They know you love them, and they love you, too. It's the same relationship we have with God.

We know that God loves us, and we love Him so dearly that it hurts us when we do something wrong. Maybe what we did wasn't intentional, but it hurts us in our spirits because we are the ones who did it.

Most things children do are unintentional; they're just children and they have to learn. That's why we need to have the Word flowing throughout our homes. Good teaching begins at home and reaches out into every area of our lives. It is the disciplining of our children and the sharing of the Scriptures with them in love that brings results.

10

Training Up
School Age Children

As time goes on, children will begin to understand that you are disciplining them because you love them. You will be not only mother and father, but friend. My girls would come home and tell me anything that was said or done at school, from elementary on up.

Sometimes it's difficult not to react. You can say things like, "I don't think that's something a child of God should be saying. I respect and love you and I don't want you saying that because I want other people to respect you." You don't have to say, "I don't want to hear that word come out of your mouth again; that's a dirty word."

Kids hear dirty words at school every day. Once a child's curiosity is aroused, he will want to hear every dirty word he can. That's how kids are. So you have to learn to use wisdom and be calm. You can act like, "I've heard that before; so what?" (Yet all the time on the inside you're thinking, "I can't believe that came out of my child's mouth.") These days children learn young. Some of the things my girls heard in elementary school were things I didn't hear until I was in junior high!

I had a teacher tell me one time that if you live through junior high without too many disasters, you've got it made. At that time I thought, "What is she talking about?" I soon learned. I praise God for the wisdom of the Word, because it sure got me out of a lot of tight places.

Don't be ashamed to say to your child, "I'm not sure of the answer now; I'm going to pray to make sure I give you the right answer." Don't say, "Well, I don't know, so don't worry about it." That's no answer—especially to a teenager.

Don't allow yourself to say, "Don't do this!" and when they ask, "Why?" say, "Because I said so!" That is not an answer. Whether or not you like what you have to say, give them an answer. If they don't get answers from you, they will go elsewhere to get them.

I have counseled teenagers who were told by their parents, "You're not old enough to understand." If children are old enough to ask, then they're old enough to understand.

When your children come to you for answers, get your Bible and express the answer in the simplest way. Then they won't go off and ask someone else.

Never raise your child to be ashamed of his body. God made the physical body. He put every part together, and every part has its own use. If it is presented to your child in that way, he will understand what the body is for, and there won't be any preconceived ideas in his mind.

So many become condemned as teenagers, because they have thoughts about their body or the bodies of others. If they are taught right, they will know where that is coming from and what to do about it. If you have taught your child properly and he is having a problem in this area, he will come to you with it.

Not only should you teach children about their bodies, you should teach them about personal hygiene. So many girls don't know anything about menstrual periods. It scares them because they don't know it's a normal thing, a part of nature. Most schools show films in gym classes, but it's much better if the girls learn about it from their mother.

Some mothers think, "They probably won't begin until they're twelve, so I'll wait until then." Don't do it! It's surprising how young some girls begin their monthly cycles.

When I became pregnant with our son, Damon, the girls were eight and ten. They were very curious and wanted to know all about it. If they want to know, you have to tell them. Get out your Bible and begin in the first chapter of Genesis. Explain that God made Adam, then saw that Adam needed a woman to make him happy. You can go from there and explain the whole thing.

It's best if they can hear these things from you. My older daughter, Candy, had a friend at school, who began telling her about her teenage sister. The sister's boyfriend would come over while her mother was at work, and the younger girl began telling Candy all that her sister and this boy did. In her terms it was unpleasant.

This happened just before I got pregnant, and it helped when I began sharing with the girls. By the way, when you share with your children, use medical terms—not slang words. If you don't know them, get a medical book.

I tried to be very open with my girls in every area. Earlier generations were very inhibited. But in the age in which we're living, it seems the Holy Spirit is drawing forth an understanding in every area of life—spirit, soul, and body.

PART IV
Woman, Wife, and Mother

11

Walking in Love

We cannot complete the study of woman, wife, and mother without stressing the importance of walking the love walk: disciplining our children in love and showing forth the Jesus kind of love to our husband. These qualities make us the Bible example of the virtuous woman and cause our home life to come in line with the Word of God.

To me, the greatest love scripture is John 3:16:

> For God so loved the world, that he gave his only begotten Son, that whosoever believeth in him should not perish, but have everlasting life.

God gave His best—His Son—that we might be free.

This illustrates a manner of living that God desires for us. Sometimes we get so caught up in our own little group. We don't allow certain ones in because they're unlovely. Perhaps they don't know God as we do.

But when God gave His Son, none were righteous. We, who have the Living God within us, must look at everyone through the eyes of love. If we are letting love become mature within us, that love reaches out. The Word says that love never fails. (1 Cor. 13:8.) People will be drawn to you just because of love.

God created us because He desired fellowship. So within every person (whether they're a new creation or not) is the desire to be loved and accepted. The only way a person understands true love is by coming into a knowledge of Jesus Christ and the Father God. When we study about love in the Word, we are seeking God Himself, because the Word says God is love. This is a vast subject.

We need to recognize that the measure of our love is the measure of our worth to society. If we feel we're not worth much to society, let's check up on our measure of love. Are we letting it flow as a force of the measure God intended?

If we feel we have worth, those around us—whether new creations or not—will feel they have worth also. We were all created by God. Those who have not been born again have worth as we do.

It is important that we have the love of God in us in full measure so that we know we are worth much to the Kingdom of God and to society. As a result, we see that the people around us are worth a great deal. God sees them through His Word—the way He wants you to see them. When you do, in any area of their life in which you can help, you let the compassion, or love, of God rise up. When this happens, you can't sit still: You have to go forth and give.

Colossians 3:14 AMP tells us: "And above all these [put on] love and enfold yourselves with the bond of perfectness—which binds everything together completely in ideal harmony."

To put on love, first, receive Jesus as your Lord and Savior. The Bible says when you receive Jesus, He and His Father come to abide with you. Together they make their home within you. The Word says God is love, so we have love to full capacity within us. The way we let that mature within us is by letting it flow and being aware of it. Love is there, and as it flows it enfolds us completely. We are enfolded in a bond of maturity that binds everything together in ideal harmony. Because God is complete, everything He does is complete.

74

God created you to be a doer. We know the motto, "Practice makes perfect." It's true. We do something over and over until we are good at it.

God expects you to be a doer of the Word. Then you will come into a maturity in the things of God and be perfected. But until you understand love, the other spiritual attributes that are supposed to abound in your life will not come to complete fruition.

God is—we are—love. We must let that love work in us in every area. A person outside of love is a failure. Why? Because he is outside of God. Anything outside of God is not complete; therefore, it will fail.

Sometimes we see someone and think, "He doesn't know God, but he's so successful. I knew him when he started in the mailroom. Now he's vice-president of the company."

We have a "pity party." We think, "I'm serving God. The Word says God prospers us in everything, but I don't have anything!"

Check yourself. Are you abounding in love?

You don't have anything, because you're not abounding in love. If you really knew that other person, you would find that he is unhappy: his home life is a disaster; his marriage is on the rocks; his children are rebellious, never having had the attention and right kind of love to build character.

So which is better: to be successful in the eyes of the world or to come into a maturity of the love of God and be successful according to the Word? The things we gain on this earth are to no avail, but the things we gain in the spiritual realm live on eternally. They are more important, because we are eternal beings.

We have to know that love is the very nature of God, and that it is alive within us. We follow forth in everything

God requires of us, because we trust him. We will never have proper trust in God unless we understand love.

There are those in the world, in darkness, who cannot understand love or allow it to flow in them. They understand only a natural love, which is selfish. It's based on performance: "If you will do this for me, I will love you. But if you won't, then forget it."

God's Love In Marriage

Many marriages do not last because they are based on natural love. The couples are not bound together in ideal harmony. *Agape* love—the love of God—is perfect; it will bind together.

Those who know God, especially those who are Spirit-filled, have no excuse for their homes to split up and their marriages to fail.

True, working to keep a marriage safe and happy is not easy. Satan always brings to our minds little details to upset us. That's why it is important to keep our minds renewed to God's Word concerning what love is and how it should work in us. Then we can make this determination: "I have the love of God within me. It is a power that binds us together. Therefore, I will let it work and flow in me. I will be a doer thereof."

We learned earlier that a Christian wife with an unsaved husband is to win him over by her manner of conversation. To do that she must let the fruit of her recreated human spirit mature and come into full bloom. Her husband will see the love of God by her manner of living.

Sometimes the circumstances may not seem better. Refuse to look at the circumstances. Let the flow of love have full course within you.

Remember this: It's not your conversation or manner of living in the natural realm that counts, but your manner of living according to Jesus Christ as Lord of your life. Let God's Word fill, engulf, and enfold you. God's nature will flow through you and become an active force within you. You and your husband will be drawn together in ideal harmony. This will not be what you have done, but what God, through you, has done.

You cannot change yourself or your mate—but God can. The Word says prayer changes things.

By letting the love of God flow through you, compassion will rise up within you. You will fall to your knees and intercede for your husband. Through that intercession, the Holy Spirit can begin working. He works not only on your husband, but on you. He shows you areas where you can do a little better. He shows you certain times when what you said or did caused your husband to react accordingly. Such things aren't always pleasant to see, but love is not an "ooshy-gooshy, sweep it all under the carpet" type of thing. Love is firm truth.

You must make this decision: "I am love; and because I am love, I will demonstrate it. Love will be effective in my life, and I will affect others with it."

Sometimes when our feelings have been hurt, we get a little bit resentful. But that's not letting the love of God mature in us. If we are letting God's love flow, we won't retaliate with natural feelings, but with God's love.

Living the Love Walk

You can go forth reconciling the world only if you're letting love be perfected in you. Otherwise, you would be looking at the world through your own eyes, not through the eyes of love. You would be limiting yourself because the knowledge you have limits you. But love has no limits.

You should confess daily: "Father, I thank You that You abide within me. Because You are love, I am love. I thank You this day, Father, that the Greater One is within me. Because You have overcome, I have overcome. Because You are a conqueror, I am more than a conqueror. I will never face a crisis alone, because You are always with me. You are there to make me a success because of love, and Your grace is that love in manifestation.''

If we have not acted in love (we're not all perfected yet), we can say, ''Father, forgive me.'' Because of grace we can repent and go on from there in His love. That is His grace in manifestation.

Here's a scripture to help perfect us in our love walk toward our brethren:

> **But we are bound to give thanks alway to God for you, brethren beloved of the Lord, because God hath from the beginning chosen you to salvation through sanctification of the Spirit and belief of the truth.**
>
> **2 Thessalonians 2:13**

So we are to thank God always for our brethren. Also, we are to recognize that their faith is exceedingly growing, just as ours should be. The love of God should be abounding among the brethren. As a result, it should gain mastery in the Church.

That is the reason you hear so much about being careful what you say about your brethren. If you say the wrong thing, you're not walking in love. It's not the one you're speaking about who will be hindered and hurt—it's you. Because love is not flowing, your faith is hindered and you're not pleasing God. The Bible says without faith it is impossible to please God. (Heb. 11:6.)

If you're not walking in full faith toward God, you're not looking in faith at anyone else. We have problems trusting people, because we haven't learned how to trust God. The area in the natural realm where we're having a problem shows us an area in the spiritual realm where we're not perfected. In that area we haven't been working for fruit to be manifested on the vine.

A fruit tree in bloom is so beautiful. But when you can see the little fruit coming out because the blossoms have fallen off, the tree isn't nearly as pretty.

After coming into the knowledge of the saving grace of Jesus Christ, we are perfect, look so beautiful, and feel so good. Knowing what God has done for us, we want to tell everybody.

Then the fruit begins to grow. That happens when we feed ourselves the Word. In the same way, a fruit tree has to be fed for it's fruit to become plump and mature.

Next bad circumstances come which we must eliminate like bugs that have to be sprayed on fruit trees. We take care of the circumstances through intercession—praying in the Spirit.

As a result of all this, fruits of righteousness come into maturity. People say, "Every time I see you, you're the same. You have a glow. The love of Jesus is all over you." The fruit being perfected within you can be seen.

You have to get close to see fruit growing. Someone relating to you on a one-to-one basis can often see that you're growing. But because many people see us only from a distance, we must let God's love work in us.

Because we see others at a distance too, perhaps we can't clearly see their fruits. We must see them as Jesus sees them—through eyes of love. We must believe God is working in them and that their faith is growing exceedingly. This lets the true love of God flow through us and come to maturity.

Always see through the eyes of love, hear through the ears of love, and do the action of love. When we do, God goes into action. We're here to reconcile people—bring them into balance—through Jesus Christ.

But we're not balanced unless we're letting the fruits of righteousness mature within us. The first fruit is love.

However, love within us is no good without action. The world is used to looking at the natural realm—looking at circumstances. When other people see no action, they think there is no love.

We have two jobs: to let our love be action so that the world can see it and to look by our spirit at our brethren, seeing them as God sees them. When we do these two things, we're allowing the full force of love to develop within us.

Confessing 1 Corinthians 13 every day will put love into action within you. By hearing and speaking it, you become aware of the love that you really are. It becomes natural to be in action.

I continually confess, "God is love and He is in me; therefore, I am love." Then basing my confession on 1 Corinthians 13 beginning with verse 4, I say, "I endure long and am patient and kind. I am never envious nor boil over with jealousy. I am not boastful or vainglorious, nor do I display myself haughtily. I am not conceited or inflated with pride.

"I am not rude and unmannerly nor do I act unbecomingly, because I am love. I am not self-seeking: I do not insist on my own way. I am not touchy, fretful, or resentful. I take no account of the evil done to me and pay no attention to a suffered wrong. I rejoice not at injustice and unrighteousness, but when right and truth prevail. I bear up under anything and everything that comes and am ever ready to believe the best of every person.

"My hopes are fadeless under all circumstances; I endure everything without weakening. I never fail, fade out, become obsolete, or come to an end."

Because God through Jesus has made me perfect, I can say I never come to an end. God says love never fails. I am love. God, an eternal being, made us eternal beings.

Therefore we never fade out or become obsolete. We have everything within us to make and keep us perfect. The body may decay and waste away, but the real me will live on forever, perfect, bound together in ideal harmony with God the Father.

As we've seen, it's important to let every fruit of righteousness become perfect unto full maturity within us. We don't wait until we're ready for the fruit to plant a fruit tree. In the same way we can't expect ourselves to bear full fruit overnight. We have the direction we need to become perfected: We must live God's Word daily.

Aren't you glad to know who you are in Christ and that God desired to create you equal with Him? Aren't you glad that He created you woman so that you can be the completing force in the natural realm as He is in the spiritual realm?

When you recognize all that is within you and what God created you to be, you can say, "God's ability is within me and I must put it to work."

We're not here to be idle, letting somebody else do our job. We're here to be ever busy—not for ourselves—but for God's Kingdom. We can work for God's Kingdom with the fullness we desire only by walking the love walk—walking in God.

We are in God, and He is in us. We must walk in Him as He desires to walk in us. Because of God's love, we become one with Him, complete in ideal harmony. His love in action in us draws others into balance. Then, like us, they become complete in Him.

12

Being Perfected
in Love

The following scripture concerning love is good teaching for young people or for those who are young in the Lord.

> Let no one despise or think less of you because of your youth, but be an example (pattern) for the believers, in speech, in conduct, in love, in faith and in purity.
>
> 1 Timothy 4:12 *AMP*

Whether your youth is physical or spiritual, don't let anyone think less of you because of it. Let God's love work through you. Instead of retaliating according to what has been said or done to you, you'll retaliate according to the Word. You'll respond according to the inward, not the outward, man. Unless we let love dominate by working through us, our physical senses dominate us.

If you can't seem to progress in certain areas because the physical senses dominate, you're not letting God's love work through you to be the dominant force.

First Peter 4:8 *AMP* states:

> Above all things have intense and unfailing love for one another, for love covers a multitude of sins—forgives and disregards the offenses of others.

That scripture is saying that if others have offended you, cover that sin. Don't publish it abroad—keep it from others' sight. That's love.

According to Luke 17:21, the Kingdom of God is inside us. We don't need to seek outside for God's joy, peace, and love. Jesus left us the Holy Spirit Who is everything we need. But we must listen to Him. The complete Trinity—God's joy, peace, and love—God's Kingdom—lives inside us.

People must understand that we don't seek God's Kingdom for things. We seek it to mature and learn its functions—how it thinks, acts, walks, and talks—so that we can function the same way.

Today, too many are concerned about things, not people. Things will vanish. But whether they are in heaven or in the pit of hell, people are eternal. Seeking God's Kingdom means seeking to help people. Seeking things is seeking self. Selfishness, which leads to pride and destruction, is not love.

By letting God express Himself through you, you can help people. God never puts anybody down: He always lifts them up. If we're walking in love, we lift people up, too.

To progress in those areas of your life that are not working out, let yourself be governed by God's love.

One day when I was studying the subject of love God said to me: "When you dam up or hinder the love that is expressing itself and flowing through you, the Word (Jesus) and the strength and power (the Holy Spirit) will not function properly through you. They are governed by love."

God's love, like a spring, needs to flow freely through us. By carrying our feelings on our shoulder and letting them get hurt, we dam up that spring spiritually. Pretty soon you can smell a stench.

Some people who dam up God's love can't figure out why nothing works in their life. The truth of the Word you give them isn't always pleasant to face. They want what's wrong with them to be somebody else's fault.

Then they let the Word begin working in them. Stirring up the gift of the Spirit within them, they pray, combining praying in the Spirit with the Word. Love begins flowing freely. It washes away the things that need to go. The spring flows into a stream flowing into a creek that flows into a river. Nothing stops the forcefully flowing river. Anything in its way is washed to the side. When we've asked forgiveness, God's love flows this same way inside us.

Once love is ruling, the Word is working in us, and faith becomes a dominating creative force. Because love brings joy and fullness, we believe and receive without effort. Love never *tries* to believe or have faith: the very word *love* suggests faith. Love makes faith limitless. God is love. When we become love, our faith becomes limitless like God's faith. Then we can reach out and help others.

Sometimes we think, *I don't want to get involved.* That is the way the world thinks. The reason we're here is to become involved with people.

Within us we have everything we need to help others. Some feel as though they're trapped inside a black hole that they can never escape. Walking in love is purity and light. People can't hurt us. But we can teach people how to be overcomers.

The Bible tells us to have intense and fervent love. Fervent suggests white heat. Different metals melt at different temperatures. Gold, being so pure, takes a white hot flame to melt it. God is telling us to have a love so forceful that it binds us together in ideal harmony.

We cannot think about accusations people may bring against us. By being unconcerned about things people say, we cover a multitude of sins. Letting the compassion of God within us flow out, we pray for the person who has offended us. The reason we're here is to let God's love flow out of us. This brings us to the awareness that we have everything we need on the inside of us.

With this working in us, we can just praise God. Walking in love and praising God stops the strife that otherwise would try to overtake us. In the strength that comes from praising God, we can walk forth as an overcomer to do whatever is necessary. With our inner man full of God's Spirit and flowing with love, we can help and strengthen others. We are on the offensive—not the defensive. Nothing can stand in our way.

We must maintain and keep God's love maturing within us by being quick to forgive, loving and living the Word, and confessing daily who we are as a love person.

Also, you can pray the following prayer in Philippians for others:

> And this I pray, that your love may abound yet more and more and extend to its fullest development in knowledge and all keen insight—that is, that your love may [display itself in] greater depth of acquaintance and more comprehensive discernment;
>
> So that you may surely learn to sense what is vital, and approve and prize what is excellent and of real value—recognizing the highest and the best, and distinguishing the moral differences; and that you may be untainted and pure and unerring and blameless, that—with hearts sincere and certain and unsullied—you may [approach] the day of Christ, not stumbling nor causing others to stumble.
>
> May you abound in and be filled with the fruits of righteousness (of right standing with God and right doing) which come through Jesus Christ, the Anointed One, to the honor and praise of God—that His glory may be both manifested and recognized.
>
> Philippians 1:9-11 *AMP*

We must develop to the fullest knowledge of love, because by this God's glory is manifested and recognized. That is why it is so important that we let the love of God flow through us and mature in us. When the Body comes into that fullness, a bond will form that cannot be broken. Everywhere we go the glory of God will be manifested and recognized.

Make a quality decision to be diligent. Discipline yourself to begin maturing in God's love. Then you can walk in God's fullness. People will see Jesus in you and have a desire to be around you. They will see love, and in love there's acceptance.

Prophecy

You've heard it said in days gone by, "How can I love? Look at my past, and the things I have done." But realize this, saith the Lord, I'm on the inside of you, and My love and ability flows out of you. So learn to flow in My ability, saith the Lord, and learn to love with My love, saith the Lord, and lay aside the things of the natural, lay aside the things of the past, and realize that the God of the universe lives within you.

I am love, saith God, and I live in you. So My ability is in you today to reach out and love others. So reach out in faith and know that faith worketh by love. My love is on the inside of you, so you are operating in My love and operating in faith, yes, even in the home area.

Yes, that one who sits by your side even now, yes, love him in Me, saith God. Yes, love her in Me, saith God. For I have given you the ability to love one another, and then the blessings of God shall flow in your place, and, yes, there shall be a love atmosphere in that place, and you'll be able to say, "Yes, it's because God lives within me, and we're operating in the God kind of love, and it has totally changed our lives."

Others will say, "Teach us how to operate in that love." And you will be a vessel used of me, saith the Lord, because of My love flowing out of you—my ability flowing out of you. Listen to Me, saith the Lord. You have it. You have it. You have it. Now operate in it.

13

Living in the
Peace of God

We must look at one more important topic to round out our study of how to reach the perfection God created us to function in as a woman. This key is walking in God's peace.

To have God's true peace, both our heart and mind must be tranquil. It's easy for our spirit to walk in peace, because Jesus, the Prince of Peace, abides there.

When Jesus hung on the cross, He suffered mental anguish. His face was unrecognizable because of all that had been mentally placed on Him. A mentally deranged person doesn't look anything like he did before his breakdown.

Jesus suffered mentally everything we ever come against. He bore all that for us. When you feel like pulling your hair out, remember that Jesus already suffered so that you can have a tranquil heart *and* mind.

We're supposed to take our place in the Body of Christ. Instead, we often let our minds run wondering, *What am I supposed to be doing? Where is my place?*

By going daily to our Father, entering the throne room, and having an intimate relationship with Him, we won't have those kinds of problems. We'll be aware of God's peace, joy, love, and faith. Ministering daily to Him will create in us a strong desire to meditate in the Word.

You meditate the Word by reading it aloud over and over so that you hear yourself speaking it forth. This leaves no room for unrest or unpeaceful thoughts. Nothing can penetrate the steadfast repetition of God's Word in your mind.

If you don't always get immediate answers to prayer, your mind isn't at peace. Your heart is alive unto God. It automatically believes everything the Word says. But the problem comes in your mind which follows the world's path of thinking. You must continually put the Word in your mind to keep it in agreement and at peace with your spirit. Then when you speak forth God's Word, it will come to pass.

Sometimes you receive what you speak with both your heart and mind, then your mind begins to think back. It wonders, *I don't know if I did that right or not. Did I do everything I was supposed to do?* Your mind received only temporarily. Bringing everything back into the natural realm keeps the words you spoke from coming to pass.

Everything that happens occurs in the spiritual before it manifests in the natural realm. This is the way God created us. God said we were made in His image. And He believes everything He says with His whole being. Therefore, the moment God speaks something, it comes to pass.

God created us like Him—spirit, soul, and body. We are a triune being. When we believe with the whole person, things happen. If they don't, usually the reason is that we're not completely at peace. We're *trying* to make the faith we have built within us work instead of *letting* it work.

We don't have to try to make our faith work—it's the God kind of faith. God says it will work if you've renewed your mind and believe His Word above everything else. When you are walking in the fullness of God, the words you speak forth automatically come to pass. Meditate on this important passage of Scripture:

Jesus answered, If a person [really] loves Me, he will keep My word—obey My teaching; and My Father will love him, and We will come to him and make Our home (abode, special dwelling place) with him.

Any one who does not [really] love Me does not observe and obey My teaching. And the teaching which you hear and heed is not Mine, but [comes] from the Father Who sent Me.

I have told you these things while I am still with you.

But the Comforter (Counselor, Helper, Intercessor, Advocate, Strengthener, Standby), the Holy Spirit, Whom the Father will send in My name [in My place, to represent Me and act on My behalf], He will teach you all things. And He will cause you to recall—will remind you of, bring to your remembrance—everything I have told you.

Peace I leave with you; My [own] peace I now give and bequeath to you. Not as the world gives do I give to you. Do not let your heart be troubled, neither let it be afraid— stop allowing yourselves to be agitated and disturbed; and do not permit yourselves to be fearful and intimidated and cowardly and unsettled.

John 14:23-27 *AMP*

Jesus says, "Peace I leave with you." He's saying:

"My peace is all you need. I have told you my Father's sayings; you know His Word. You're supposed to be doing that Word. Even though I'm going away, you will continue to know.

"If you have kept everything I have told you in your heart—if it has become a part of you because you are doing it—the Holy Spirit, Whom the Father is sending in My place, will bring all those things to remembrance.

"Don't let circumstances take My peace from you; they cannot. Walk in My peace. That is all you need."

Isn't that simple? Because peace passes all understanding, the world cannot take it away.

Jesus tells us that being agitated and disturbed can affect our spirit. By not renewing our mind, we let ourselves become agitated, cowardly, intimidated, disturbed, and unsettled. This goes against and eventually causes confusion in our spirit man. That's when we get in trouble. God is not the author of confusion. (1 Cor. 14:33.) *We* must do something about the confusion.

Some people continually want others to do the work and teachings of Jesus for them. God has always desired that His Church march forth as a strong army. He wants every member of the Church doing His work, walking in His peace. This includes some slothful people who go from one meeting to another, getting spiritually fat, but never acting on the Word. God said to me, "It grieves Me because this has delayed My coming."

Some go to the other extreme. They run around trying to do too many things. Worn out, they become ineffective. We need to learn balance—in that, we will find peace.

Have you ever caught yourself suddenly becoming agitated? Let me give you an example.

Once when we were redoing our North Worship Hall, I was in charge of the decorating. Because Buddy and I were out of town a lot, I left a list of things I wanted done—when, where, and how.

On Sunday I was there to minister to the people—I didn't look at the physical plant. But on Monday morning when I walked in, I began to look.

One day I became more and more agitated and irritated the further I walked down a hallway. Some things on the list either hadn't been done according to my instructions, or hadn't been done at all. At the end of the hallway I thought: *Satan, you're not going to rob me of my peace, because Isaiah 9 says that Jesus came as my Prince of Peace. Because Jesus abides within me, I have peace. According to John 14, Jesus said that He left His peace with me and the world cannot take it away. Therefore, Satan, you cannot take it away.* Then I began to pray in tongues.

God's peace rose up from the inside of me—from where He lives. Calmly, I turned around and went back down the hall to find out what had happened.

One thought Satan had come against me with was this: *You are a woman; the workers are men. You can't go up to them and say, "Why didn't you do this right?" They know what they're doing.*

I may not have known how to do a particular thing, but I knew what I wanted. When I related to the men what I wanted, they should have done it. Instead of being intimidated because I was a woman, I was walking in the peace of God.

Calmly, quietly, and in God's love, I questioned the men. "Why was this wallpaper put here when it was supposed to be there? Why was this trim stained the wrong color? Why was this job not done last week?"

By speaking in God's love this way, you keep yourself from becoming disturbed, agitated, and intimidated. You walk in the peace of God.

Prophecy

So don't be moved by the extraneous things that happen in your life. Be moved by the faith that's on the inside, and rest in the peace it brings.

It makes no difference how things appear to be. You know what My Word has to say, you know what you've spoken, and you know it's got to conform, and go that way.

And so the peace of God and the rest of God should be that which keeps your hearts and minds, so you're not always getting agitated and reacting. People who react to what's on the outside don't have My highest and best. Peace doesn't react instantly: it's always at rest. It has acted beforehand on the Word which is true, and if you do that, peace will work for you.

When the telephone rings, don't panic, just say, "I'll be with you later. I'm going to spend time with my Father first." Then the peace of God will keep you no matter what the news might have been, because to make haste and react is sin. But

93

to walk in faith and peace, this is good and right. It will keep you in the right way.

So begin your day by walking in peace every day. That way it will continue all day long. Don't wait until the middle of the afternoon when everything begins to go wrong. Start early and continue therein. Everything will work for good, because the peace of God is keeping you like it should.

Conclusion

When we function as adaptable, suitable, and completing helpers to our husbands, we are fulfilled in our marriages. When we teach our children properly in the Word and live the Word before them, we are fulfilled with beautiful children.

Seek God first by interceding for and tending to your family. Abound in love and walk in God's peace—be a virtuous woman. Your husband will be proud of you, and your children will call you blessed. You'll realize how beautiful it is that God skillfully and carefully handcrafted you to be desired and admired.

Aren't you glad God created you a woman?

Pat Harrison is a woman of God who follows after love. A frequent speaker at women's sessions and seminars, she moves in the flow of the office of the prophet and is very sensitive to the Holy Spirit.

With wisdom and understanding, she ministers powerfully on the love of God, exhorting the Body of Christ to let God's love be perfected in them. Her desire is to lift up Jesus that all men would come to know Him.

Pat and her husband, Rev. Buddy Harrison, have traveled around the world bringing light to the dark and love to the unloved. As a couple, they have ministered to churches and organizations on three continents. Her simplicity in teaching God's truth refreshes and encourages people.

Pat is the mother of three beautiful children, a son and two daughters, and the proud grandmother of three.

For a list of cassette tapes by
Pat Harrison
or for other information,
write:

Pat Harrison
P. O. Box 35443
Tulsa, OK 74153

Please include your prayer requests
and comments when you write.

Books by Pat Harrison

Learning the Ways of the Holy Spirit
His Indwelling Presence
and His Outpouring Power

Woman, Wife, Mother

Available from your local bookstore.

HARRISON HOUSE
P. O. Box 35035
Tulsa, OK 74153

In Canada contact:

Word Alive
P. O. Box 284
Niverville, Manitoba
CANADA R0A 1E0

For International sales in Europe,
contact:

Harrison House Europe
Belruptstrasse 42 A
A — 6900 Bregenz
AUSTRIA